Horns

by the

Bull

Does the bull have you,
or do you have the bull?

2365 Rice Blvd., Suite 202
Houston, Texas 77005

ISBN: 978-0-9915511-0-1

10   9   8   7   6   5   4   3   2   1

Library of Congress Cataloging-in-Publication Data on file with publisher.

Editorial Direction, Lucy Herring Chambers
Creative Direction, Ellen Peeples Cregan
Design, Marla Y. Garcia

Printed in Canada through Friesens

Horns
by the
Bull

Does the bull have you,
or do you have the bull?

RICK BATY

rule2books

Table
of Contents

Introduction

When was the last time that you couldn't wait for tomorrow because you just knew that something good was on its way? You were singing in the rain, dancing on the ceiling, and laughing so hard that it made you cry.

But when that day came, it wasn't anything like what you were anticipating. The rain was not the soft pitter-patter on your umbrella, but more the torrential downpour that ended up flooding your house. The music you were dancing to was suddenly silenced long before you were ready for it to be over. Your laughter was replaced with an overwhelming sense of disappointment, confusion, and anger. The high hopes of tomorrow were brutally dashed with a second's notice.

Well, that's my story. At least part of it. And my guess is that it may very well be yours as well. We've all had those wonderful days when the sun shone brightly on our life. But all too quickly the sunshine turned to rain. More rain than we ever expected to see. The harsh reality of living in this world is that each and every one of us experiences times that we just are not ready for. Times when we're blind-sided by events, people, and circumstances we never anticipated.

That's why it is so important to learn how to cultivate a Plan B, and dust off your britches, and rise above the rubble of your shattered dreams. It's lonely out there, and it's easy to feel like you're the only one who has ever felt this disappointed, this betrayed, this hopeless. But the reality is that there are a lot more folks out there in your boat than you might think. And hopefully at least some of them are paddling with you.

Is your boat floating or is it sinking? Is it balanced or is it making ripples? And just exactly how do you dig deep and keep paddling? Or perhaps even more importantly, how do you change your route? Fact is, your life will be forever changing; and none of us can predict the future. What we can do, though, is live each day as if it were our last.

That's what this book is all about. Discovering

how to fully enjoy the good times when they come and how to handle the bad times as well. Most of all, it's about attacking life rather than merely existing. Sometimes you just have to take the bull by the horns. But what about the times when the bull has you, and you're on the receiving end of the horns? That's what we'll be looking at throughout our journey together—how to regain our grasp on the bull's horns in spite of setbacks, failures, and even disaster. So as we begin, let me ask you a question: Does the bull have you or do you have the bull?

CHAPTER I

A Great Foundation

*G*rowing up I got to see every kind of lifestyle you could imagine. I was very fortunate to be raised in a middle-class family in Houston, Texas. As a kid, I experienced wild, wonderful, and even dangerous things. I was able to expand my imagination and develop my creativity *doing stuff that you would never be able to do today. I think my most favorite memories come from the years I was ten to thirteen. I learned many things, saw many things, and tried many things. These were great years, indeed. Years that helped lay the foundation for the rest of my life. Of course I didn't realize that at the time.*

Many of the most powerful lessons came from my very best friend—my grandpa. He was the head custodian for South Houston High School until he retired to Wheelock, Texas, with my grandma who had been a nurse at St. Joseph Hospital. There they lived on one hundred acres that had been passed down through Grandpa's family from as far back as the 1800's. I had the great privilege and joy of spending most of my summers there.

During those summers I learned how important the simple life was and how much I wanted to be like my grandparents. Although it was a simple life, it was also one that involved much hard work. So much hard work that I realized that I did not want to do that the rest of my life! Every Sunday, everyone came to have lunch at Grandma's at twelve o'clock sharp. And I mean everyone! Those Sunday lunches were often the highlight of my week. There was so much laughing, so much playing, and such great food. I learned that the simple fun of being with friends and family around great food could be the best fun there was.

My grandparents' home was a simple affair, a one-room house that had a bed, a porch, and a big iron stove. It also had an outhouse and a well where we pumped our water. The stove kept us warm and cooked our meals. We had coal oil lamps to give us light, and a variety of homemade remedies to take care of aches, pains, ticks, and chiggers. I had chores like feeding the cows, getting the eggs, and helping in the garden. I also got to cut weeds with my grandpa's old Farm All. It was his baby, and I got to drive it. I also had a three-speed 1947 Willys Jeep that became my farm truck when I was twelve. Can you imagine that? Being able to drive around the farm on my own at twelve? It doesn't get much better than that for a Houston city boy. It was my big release.

I also had the responsibility of keeping my two second cousins in sight; both of them had Down syndrome. Willy was tough but couldn't talk. Tim could talk, but not well. He would give just a little chuckle showing he approved. I knew what he was saying, as did my grandma and his mother, but not many others could understand him. He would ride horses, and you could tell that's when he felt his greatest comfort; just like I did driving my Willys Jeep. Tim also had a mind to do it his way, and that was fine with me. If you bucked him, he would buck you. I always tried to take his mind to the limit, to stretch him, but it was important to know his limits.

From ten to thirteen, I drove trucks, mended fences, plowed fields, and saw life in ways few could ever imagine. When I tell people about those days, many of them can't believe me—even my wife. I got so used to getting light from coal oil lamps that to this day light bulbs are difficult for me. I had a great horse; she was a Shetland pony named Dolly. Riding Dolly, I first began rehearsing what would one day become my freeway speeches. I had a plan every time I got on that pony. I was a huge fan of Bonanza,

The Rifleman, and The High Chaparral. On every ride, I felt I was a character in those shows. I developed and rehearsed my speeches every day on my pony. Those were great days to be alive.

Do you have a "Bucket List" or a "Wish List?" I never did. I just did all these things, and later I decided that they should have been on my "Bucket List." Not many people feel that way about their experiences.

Something else was happening during those days on the farm. Preparation. The speeches I made on Dolly prepared me to give the same kind of speeches today. The speeches are simpler now, and the characters are real. I'll explain more about the speeches later, but for now it's important to know that those days of honest, hard work laid the foundation that helped me get through the tough times of adulthood.

Learning how to care for my second cousins was invaluable training for learning how to genuinely care for all people, whatever their station in life. As an adult, I was in the habit of drinking my coffee and reading my newspaper before beginning work each morning. I always bought the paper from a man named James at the corner of Ella and 610, right by my office. My wife would often call around the time I would be pulling into the office and ask if I had bought my paper yet. I would tell her that I had. "Why do you always buy a paper from James?" she would ask. And I would respond, "Because that could easily be me out there selling those papers." My experience with my second cousins had helped mold how I would see people the rest of my life. It's funny how life works: You never know how what you are going through is going to help you in the future. You just know that it will.

I was truly blessed with a great foundation. As I've continued to build my house along the way, certain truths, which I've come to call "The Other Ten Commandments," have helped me stay centered upon that foundation. Here they are:

The Other Ten Commandments

1. Prayer is not a spare wheel that you pull out when in trouble, but is a steering wheel that directs the right path throughout life.

2. Why is a car's windshield so large and its rear

view mirror so small? Because our past is not as important as our future. So, look ahead and move on.

3. Friendship is like a book. It takes a few seconds to burn, but it takes years to write.

4. All things in life are temporary. If things are going well, enjoy it; they will not last forever. If things are going wrong, don't worry: they can't last long either.

5. Old friends are gold. New friends are diamonds. If you get a diamond, don't forget the gold! Because to hold a diamond, you always need a base of gold.

6. Often when we lose hope and think "This is the end," God smiles from above and says, "Relax, sweetheart, it's just a bend, not the end!"

7. When God solves your problems, you have faith in His abilities; when God doesn't solve your problems He has faith in your abilities.

8. A blind person asked St. Anthony: "Can there be anything worse than losing eye sight?" He replied: "Yes, losing your vision!"

9. When you pray for others, God listens to you

and blesses them. When you are safe and happy, someone has prayed for you.

10. Worrying doesn't take away tomorrow's troubles; it takes away today's peace.

Keeping these thoughts in mind have created a strong fence around my family's life that has helped keep the bull from getting us. I hope you'll find them just as helpful.

CHAPTER II

Smooth Sailing

I love the ocean and the smell of the fresh sea breeze. In particular, I love the beauty of watching the day begin as the sun peaks over the horizon and the life of the sea comes alive. I relish those days when I have been able to walk the shore, looking for elusive game fish *and finding myself able to forget all else that surrounds me. I have had many wonderful times on the bay with friends and family; times that have helped create the best of stories. One thing I've learned over the years is that good times and smooth sailing don't last forever. At least not in this life.*

I remember the time when I was on the cruise of a lifetime. A beautiful ship took us to ports of call that I had only read about or seen in magazines. The black tie affairs each evening were lavish; they seemed just like the best parties on the Titanic. Life couldn't get any better. But as it happened with the Titanic, the unthinkable lay right around the corner.

Before I tell you the rest of the story, let me ask you to do something. Imagine yourself for a moment being on the big blue sea enjoying a spectacular cruise into the sunset. You're looking back fondly on what a wonderful day it has been. The music is playing and you're having the time of your life when suddenly—unexpectedly—you fall off the boat and plunge into the dark water of the sea. You feel tremendous anguish as you see the boat go on without you. The music fades, and the light disappears. But this is just the beginning of the pain you are about bear. Now, you're all alone; there is nothing but you and the sea. It's a situation you never, ever expected to be in. And it is a time when you will have to make choices—and good ones, at that—or the sea will get you.

All of us have times in our lives which could be best described as "smooth sailing," I like to describe these times as, "I'm just loving and living." These are those wonderful periods where we can genuinely say, "Life is good." Very good, in fact. Maybe it's the honeymoon period after you're first married, the excitement and opportunity of your first job, the thrill of your first child or grandchild, that new sports car, the club championship, the special award or promotion. These are the days of the magic-carpet ride—days we hope will never end.

But, if I've learned anything in my fifty plus years of life on this planet it's this: Smooth sailing is not forever. Sooner or later every one of us falls off the boat. Like you, I've fallen off more than a few times. There was the day when we moved during my eighth grade year and overnight I lost my closest friends whom I had grown up with; the day when my best friend—my grandpa–passed away; and the day when I was blindsided by the loss of my job. For you, falling off the boat may be the loss of a loved one, a devastating illness, financial collapse, an unexpected and unwanted divorce, or betrayal by a very close friend.

Sooner or later we all hit the cold waters of unexpected tragedy and unfair treatment. The question then becomes, "How do I stay afloat?" I don't mean financially primarily, I mean keeping your head on straight and finding your way to the shore. You have to swim, because there is no one out there to throw you a life jacket. And it's not an easy swim, for sure. Along the way, hopefully you'll have some friends who will come out to see how you're doing, offer support, and tell you how much they understand, even though they usually won't. They have good intentions, but in situations like these, they just don't have a big enough jacket to keep you afloat.

I plunged headlong into the icy waters of unexpected disaster from my job of over twenty years. I had worked my way up to become the fourth largest shareholder in the second largest insurance agency in Houston. I had been the largest producer for this firm each year for the past ten years. It wasn't always easy, by any measure, but I was riding the wave of success and enjoying the smooth sailing of a profitable, successful life. I was lucky; I had a wonderful wife and two great little girls whom we adopted. I loved all of them deeply.

But deep down, I smelled a rat. I can't explain exactly why, but I just knew. When you feel a warning in your gut, you may not know what it is, but, chances are, it's telling you to watch out for something. And something was stirring at my firm. I felt it, but I didn't want to react until I knew exactly what it was. The first seven years at this firm were some of the best business days of my life. I drank the Kool-Aid, and lots of it. But then the taste began to change, and I didn't like it as much. Each time I took a deep drink, instead of feeling the coolness and being refreshed, I got that feeling that things weren't right. In fact, things were very wrong. There were things going on, and they knew that I knew. My dad had always told me, "Don't better yourself at the expense of others," and I was seeing exactly that. The practices I was becoming aware of at the firm were just wrong.

First, I wanted all the facts. Second, I wanted to catch my partners at their game. But before I had that opportunity, perhaps their own instincts told them that I was on to something. So they were kind enough to send my wife and me on a great trip on an amazing ship in that big blue sea, the Mediterranean. In Portofino, Italy, while I was having a crisp glass of wine and a pizza, it hit me. Fancy boat, great ports of call, lavish black-tie parties every night. "Oh my God," I said as my sun-tanned face went white. My wife thought I was having a heart attack. It wasn't physical, but as I suddenly realized what had happened, it was wrenching: We had been set up.

When I returned to my office, I found all my drawers empty. They had cleaned me out. I was fired from the very firm I had helped take to the top. I was devastated. The inner pain seemed unbearable. I couldn't sleep for nights. I couldn't eat and lost quite a bit of weight. I always made sure that none of my neighbors were walking their dogs when I went out to get the morning newspaper, because I didn't want them to see me crying or throwing up in the bushes. I scheduled breakfast with two different people at the same place at the same time, and I still can't remember why I set the meetings or what I wanted to talk about. I was a wreck, pure and simple. And it didn't look like there were any lifeboats around to keep me from going under.

One of the most difficult parts of the situation was how it affected the people around me whom I cared for deeply. My wife and daughters, at the time eight and nine, were crushed as they saw my ongoing pain. Unfortunately, I wasn't seeing their pain. Then one day, as we headed to the airport for a family trip, my younger daughter broke down in tears as we drove by the building where I used to say "Hey girls, that's where Daddy works." It was eight months later, and the pain had been building up for them. When we got to the airport my wife asked me, "Are you ok?" I said, "No. This has had more of an effect on our family than I realized." They had been my lifejackets, and they were keeping me afloat. But they were paying a higher price than I had understood.

Today things are much better. But it didn't happen overnight. Getting back up and getting back in the game is never an overnight affair. But it's a critical part of life for everyone. And what I want to share with you are the lessons and principles that helped me get back on my feet and grab the bull by the horns again.

Perhaps you find yourself in a similar situation. Maybe it's not quite as devastating, or perhaps it's even more so. Whatever the current details of your life, one thing is sure: Life is an ongoing adventure made up of days of smooth sailing interrupted by plunges into the icy waters. And there are many days that seem sort of in-between. But when we inevitably hit the waters, we've got to know how to get back into the boat, how to make good choices for bad times, as I like to put it. How can you do it? Stay focused, remember your true values, and most of all, never forget who brought you to the dance.

CHAPTER III

The Best Lunch I Ever Had

I know you've heard the saying, "You are what you eat." Well, it could also be said, "You are what you hear." One of the best lunches I ever had wasn't so memorable because of the chicken fried steak and mashed potatoes in front of me, but because of the person sitting across the table.

Shortly after my corporate divorce, a dear friend invited me to have lunch with one of his friends. My friend was trying to throw me a lifejacket. He had heard bits and pieces of my saga from others who knew me, but now he got to hear my "poor, pitiful me" story from the horse's mouth. I'm not sure why this man took the time, or why I felt compelled to give him the play-by-play of what had happened to me; but he was nice enough to listen as I spewed my pain and anger. After I was through, he said, "May I ask you a question?" I said, "Sure." I was totally unprepared for the question he asked. He said, "Will you ever forgive them?" Wow. I told him that I had never considered forgiveness, and that, quite frankly, it was too early in the process. I still hadn't gotten the bad taste out of my mouth. Whether it was malice, intent to deceive, or just flat lying, the situation didn't settle well with me, as it wouldn't have with most folks I know.

He looked at me intently and said quietly but passionately, "I have a story for you. It's about my wife. While she was driving down FM 1960 in Houston a drunk hit her and her father head on and killed her dad. The man was convicted and went to prison for two years. However, she couldn't get the anger out of her mind and heart. She would wake up every day mad at the world and have that 'poor, pitiful me' syndrome.

"Then one day she woke up, got out of bed, and said, 'I can't live like this anymore. I have to forgive this person or this pain inside will kill me.' Believe it or not, she called him, and they had lunch that day and she forgave him for what he did to her and her family." Suddenly, my story didn't seem so big any more. I learned a life-altering, joy-restoring lesson that day: Sometimes you just have to bury whatever it is and move on.

People make bad choices, and, trust me, they are living with the consequences and guilt of those choices. But as someone has said, "Don't let anger eat you up by refusing to forgive the one who has wronged you."

I'll never forget that lunch. It was the jump start I needed to begin forgiving those who had wronged me. And it was the start of getting back into the boat. My guess is that you have people in your life that have wronged you, perhaps badly, perhaps intentionally. The longer you hold onto bitterness and hatred toward them, the longer your soul will pay the price. It costs to forgive, believe me I know. But in the end it costs more not to forgive. A friend of mine sent me a quote by Frederick Buechner that puts it as well as I've ever heard.

> Of the Seven Deadly Sins, anger is possibly the most fun. To lick your wounds, to smack your lips over grievances long past, to roll over your tongue the prospect of bitter confrontations still to come, to savor to the last toothsome morsel both the pain you are given and the pain you are giving back — in many ways it is a feast fit for a king. The chief drawback is that what you are wolfing down is yourself. The skeleton at the feast is you.

As someone else said of un-forgiveness, "It's a game that can't be won, only played." Every day that is spent with bitterness and un-forgiveness is a day of missed happiness. And our days are severely numbered…so put joy in your life. Genuine forgiveness is one of the most difficult aspects of breaking free of the horns by the bull—and one of the most important. Perhaps there is someone you need to have lunch with. Don't put it off any longer; it may well be the best lunch you ever have.

CHAPTER IV

We're Not That Different

I'd like to tell you something that I think you already know. There is a very fine line between you and me. A very, very fine line. We think more alike than either of us probably would ever imagine. We each have a multitude of similar experiences and probably just as *many similar behaviors. Fact is, we relate to one another more than not. True, we are probably quite different in many ways. But what we're not different in is that you and I are both thoroughly and completely human. We are on the same journey together, made of the same stuff for that journey, experiencing so many of the same ups and downs of this journey. At least that's how it seems to me.*

Why do I believe this? Well, how many times have you heard someone relate a story that makes you think, "Man, the exact same thing happened to me." Or someone tells you about something they were wondering about and you say to yourself, "Yeah, me too." Our humanity joins us together in the experiences of life more tightly than we probably ever realize.

I was at a club I belonged to one day having lunch by myself, as I often do. But this time was different. A gentleman came up to my table and asked if he could sit down. I'm like Will Rogers who once said,

"I never met a man I didn't like," so I said, "Sure, have a seat." He proceeded to tell me something I wasn't expecting. He said, "Son, I've been watching you come into this club and this locker room for some years. You've always had a smile on your face and would strike up a conversation with anyone. Lately I haven't seen that smile or those colorful conversations." He continued on, "I'm going to tell you a story about a man who had this big 'ole house in Aspen, Colorado. He gets a call one day from his banker who tells him he is closing his line of credit. A few hours later he gets another call from his wife who tells him she is leaving and filing for divorce." I told him that other than the banker and the wife, that story sound just like mine.

He said, "I know. I've heard your story, and the one I just told you is mine. Now what I'm going to tell you, son, is what I had to do. Go home and polish those shoes to where they have a perfect shine. Get some brass cleaner and make those buttons on your jacket gleam as bright as the day you first wore them. Put the starch back into your shirt and put a smile on your face. Son, look like a million if you only have a penny. It will all come back to you." That day I received a life jacket from a fellow deep-water survivor. His advice helped me navigate the difficult waters of my experience.

We are more alike than probably most of us realize. However there is one difference, a very real and important difference. While our experiences may often be the same, our response to these situations can vary dramatically. Similar experiences and similar thoughts don't guarantee similar responses, by a long shot. One person is wronged badly by a close friend, and they feel all the hurt and betrayal that goes along with that. But they choose to forgive that friend nonetheless. Another person is wronged just as badly and feels the exact same hurt and betrayal as the first. But this person chooses not to forgive and becomes angry and bitter. Same circumstance, same internal experience, but dramatically different responses. If you were to ask me if I ever struggle with being bitter or angry, I would be lying if I told you no. But I'm more at ease today because time will take the edge off.

And that puts all of the ingredients into what

helps create our personality. But here comes the hard part: Admitting it! You have issues. I have issues. Everyone, everyone, has issues. Having problems is part of being human. And guess what? We all have our demons. Yes, you have demons, and they are pulling and tugging on you every day. So do I. Not literal demons, of course, though sometimes it may feel like it. But all of us have dark parts of ourselves that we wish weren't there and certainly don't want others to find out about. The dark parts come with belonging to the human race.

My preacher told me something critical to remember: You will never change anyone. These issues that we call demons are all part of our makeup, our chemistry, our inner world. The sooner you recognize this and learn how to accept them for who they are and what they are, the sooner you will find calm within yourself. It doesn't matter if other people are not being honest about their own demons and issues. Some people say they love everybody. They're either lying or they're choosing not to be honest about their inner world. It took me a long time to come to this understanding. I wish I had realized it earlier and could have had the patience and balance it brings all my life.

I've come to realize that whether what I wished for didn't happen, or whether what I did not wish for did happen; everything happens for a reason. When we can just understand that somehow, somewhere there is ultimately a reason for whatever happened; then we can get through whatever we're facing. Everyone has demons. You can't change that. But can you forgive the person who wronged you? Can you handle your own demons?

Find joy in your life and peace within yourself, and you will be wealthier than most of the rich people I know. But you have to know how to find these treasures. Language experts say that most people speak about one hundred and fifty to two hundred words every minute. But we talk to ourselves at about thirteen hundred words a minute. All that self-talk can powerfully impact on your emotions, causing stress or low self-esteem. How do you control this inner nagging? You have to recognize it, challenge it, and replace it with a positive inner voice. You can't indulge yourself in saying negative things about yourself or about others. If you find yourself thinking negatively, replace those thoughts with something kind and positive.

Most of the time, it's just a matter of perspective. I tell folks that my senior year in high school I played quarterback and we were 5 and 5. We lost five at home and five on the road. Never say you were 0-10. It was an incredibly humbling and embarrassing time. There were twelve men on the team and I was the twelfth. The coach would make me walk up and down the sideline with him, handling the phone set. Finally I got my friends in the stands to start chanting, "We want Baty! We want Baty!" Coach finally said, "Baty, go up in the stands and see what those folks want." When I told him, he finally put me in the game. He told me to run four plays at quarterback. On the first down I was to run around the right end. On the second down I was to run around the left end. Third down I was to drop back and run a quarterback draw. On the fourth down I was to punt.

On the first play we were on our own twenty-yard line, and I ran around right end to pick up twenty yards. Now the ball was on the forty. The next play I ran around left end and managed to pick up another twenty yards. The ball was on their forty. On the third play, I ran the quarterback draw and got the ball all the way to the one yard line. As the coach had instructed me, on the fourth play I dropped back and punted the ball out of the stadium. Coach brought me to the sideline, grabbed my facemask, and screamed, "What the hell were you thinking?" I said, "I was thinking that we had the dumbest coach I've ever seen in all my life!"

I had so many expectations of myself, as did everyone in our small town. But guess what? Those losses made big winners out of several players on my team. I have seen nine starters on that team become top professionals in their field. I know another team that won the state championship and doesn't have anywhere near that same percentage of profession-als in their class. It's up to each of us to get back up after we've failed, dust ourselves off, and learn what we can from each defeat. You can choose to focus on your ten losses, or you can get a better perspective and move forward to new victories.

CHAPTER V

The Four O'clock Brainstorm

*I*t happens more often than we'd like. We find ourselves awakened from a night's sleep only to discover that it's too early to get up, but we're too awake to fall back to sleep. And one of the biggest problems is that we can't remember what just woke us up. But this frustrating *situation can become one of the most important parts of our day. It's what I like to call the four o'clock brainstorm.*

Some of my best thoughts occur when I am horizontal on my bed at four in the morning. I'm not saying I can solve the world's problems lying horizontally with less than eight hours of sleep, but at 4:30 a.m. my best thinking of the day is taking place. Ideas fit together to solve problems as though I knew the answer all along. I am my freshest, even if a bit sleepy. There is something about those early morning hours that puts my mind in a relaxed and productive mode.

I have put some of my best thoughts together at this time. One of the main reasons is that the only one listening to my theory is me. I have found it helpful to pick up the phone and call my voice mail with those early morning strategies, thoughts, and, especially, dreams. By capturing these clear thoughts, I have a much better chance of putting them into action during the day. Try it next time you find yourself awake at four in the morning. I believe you'll find some great inspiration, if you'll just record it.

I have started a few companies in my time, and all but one has seen success. The only one that failed was not part of the early morning dreaming. So let me ask you a question. What is in your dream? Can you describe its details or the path it is heading down? The stark reality is that if you don't harness those thoughts and dreams down–whether we write them down, call our voice mail, or find another way to record them–what you envision most likely will not happen. There are so many distractions, pressures, and challenges during the day that your early morning gems will be lost if you don't guard them jealously. I encourage you to make sure to record them as soon as they come to you. It's amazing how easily and quickly the great ideas we have become lost with the passing of time.

When I consider all the puzzles I've pieced together with four o'clock brainstorms, I realize something else very important: These ideas only become reality if we have the huevos to do something about them, if we have the courage to take the risk and go for broke in pursuing our dreams. Don't look back and say, "Man, if I only would have done it the way I imagined." Rather, say—in the immortal words of Frank Sinatra—"I did it my way."

Trying to stick square pegs in round holes will create frustration that will make you look back one day and say, "Shame on me for not taking the risk that would have finally put the square peg in the square hole." Only one thing is worse than discovering our dream was a failure, and that's to stop dreaming. If you don't have challenges and dreams that wake you up in the early morning or keep you awake at night, then probably one of three things has happened. One, you're already there and you are enjoying the rich rewards of having pursued your dream success-fully. Great, enjoy it. Two, you are in the process of discovering your next dream and haven't quite found it. That's fine; just don't stop looking. Or three, your body is so tired you just don't have the strength to care about your next dream. We all have times like that. But once you get your strength back, don't forget to go back to dreaming.

One final word here: Test the waters, but also

know your limitations. There is no valor in going after something that is simply beyond your resources and abilities. Know your risk tolerance; it varies from individual to individual. The law of economics states that without risk there is no return. And that's exactly right. But everyone has to discover the level of risk-taking that they can handle.

I never want to look back with regrets, but I do want to capitalize on my mistakes. Regrets can make you lose sleep and may even make you lose your four o'clock brainstorming sessions. But capitalizing on mistakes is the best way to make your way out of the mire of regret. We all make mistakes, and I hope you learn everything you can from them, as I have tried to do. The old saying holds true; we don't want to jump over the fence and get bit by the same dog. Keeping notes at four o'clock in the morning is a great way to keep that from happening!

CHAPTER VI

Steps To The Top

*D*ave Kerpen, the bestselling author and CEO, has written a tremendous article called 11 Simple Concepts to Become a Better Leader. I think you'll find these ideas incredibly helpful.

1. **Listening** *"When people talk, listen completely. Most people never listen."* - ERNEST HEMINGWAY

   Listening is the foundation of any good relationship. Great leaders listen to what their customers and prospects want and need, and they listen to the challenges those customers face. They listen to colleagues and are open to new ideas. They listen to shareholders, investors, and competitors.

2. **Storytelling** *"Storytelling is the most powerful way to put ideas into the world today."*

   – ROBERT MCAFEE BROWN

   After listening, leaders need to tell great stories in order to sell their products, but more importantly, in order to sell their ideas. Storytelling is what captivates people and drives them to take action. Whether you're telling a story to one prospect over lunch, a boardroom full of people, or thousands of people through an online video, storytelling wins customers.

3. **Authenticity** *"I had no idea that being your authentic self could make me as rich as I've become. If I had, I'd have done it a lot earlier."* – OPRAH WINFREY

Great leaders are who they say they are, and they have integrity beyond compare. Vulnerability and humility are hallmarks of the authentic leader and create a positive, attractive energy. Customers, employees, and media all want to help an authentic person to succeed. There used to be a divide between one's public self and private self, but the social internet has blurred that line. Tomorrow's leaders are transparent about who they are online, merging their personal and professional lives together.

4. **Transparency** *"As a small businessperson, you have no greater leverage than the truth."*

   – JOHN WHITTIER

   There is nowhere to hide anymore, and businesspeople who attempt to keep secrets will eventually be exposed. Openness and honesty lead to happier staff and customers and colleagues. More important, transparency makes it a lot easier to sleep at night—unworried about what you said to whom, a happier leader is a more productive one.

5. **Team Playing** *"Individuals play the game, but teams beat the odds."* – SEAL TEAM SAYING

No matter how small your organization, you interact with others every day. Letting others shine, encouraging innovative ideas, practicing humility, and following other rules for working in teams will help you become a more likeable leader. You'll need a culture of success within your organization, one that includes out-of-the-box thinking.

6. **Responsiveness** *"Life is 10% what happens to you and 90% how you react to it."* – CHARLES SWINDOLL

The best leaders are responsive to their customers, staff, investors, and prospects. Every stakeholder today is a potential viral sparkplug, for better or for worse, and the winning leader is one who recognizes this and insists upon a culture of responsiveness. Whether the communication is email, voice mail, a note or a tweet, responding shows you care and gives your customers and colleagues a say, allowing them to make a positive impact on the organization.

7. **Adaptability** *"When you're finished changing, you're finished."* – BEN FRANKLIN

There has never been a faster-changing marketplace than the one we live in today. Leaders must be flexible in managing changing opportunities and challenges and nimble enough to pivot at the right moment. Stubbornness is no longer desirable to most organizations. Instead, humility and the willingness to adapt mark a great leader.

8. **Passion** *"The only way to do great work is to love the work you do."* – STEVE JOBS

Those who love what they do don't have to work a day in their lives. People who are able to bring passion to their business have a remarkable advantage, as that passion is contagious to customers and colleagues alike. Finding and increasing your passion will absolutely affect your bottom line.

9. **Surprise and Delight** *"A true leader always keeps an element of surprise up his sleeve, which others cannot grasp but which keeps his public excited and breathless."* – CHARLES DE GAULLE

Most people like surprises in their day-to-day lives. Likeable leaders under-promise and over-deliver, assuring that customers and staff are surprised in a positive way. There are a plethora of ways to surprise without spending extra money.

10. **Simplicity** *"Less isn't more; just enough is more."* – MILTON GLASER

The world is more complex than ever before, and yet what customers often respond to best is simplicity—in design, form, and function. Taking complex projects, challenges, and ideas and distilling them to their simplest components allows customers, staff, and other stakeholders to better understand and buy into your vision. We humans all crave simplicity, and so today's leader must be focused and deliver simplicity.

11. **Gratefulness** *"I would maintain that thanks are the highest form of thought, and that gratitude is happiness doubled by wonder."*

– GILBERT CHESTERTON

Likeable leaders are ever grateful for the people who contribute to their opportunities and success. Being appreciative and saying thank you to mentors, customers, colleagues, and other stakeholders keeps leaders humble, appreciated, and well-received. It also makes you feel great! Donor's Choose studied the value of a hand-written thank-you note, and actually found donors were 38% more likely to give a second time if they received a hand-written note.

The Golden Rule: Above all else, treat others as you'd like to be treated. By showing others the same courtesy you expect from them, you will gain more respect from coworkers, customers, and business partners. Holding others in high regard demonstrates your company's likeability and motivates others to work with you. This seems so simple, as do so many of these principles—and yet many people, too concerned with making money or getting by, fail to truly adopt these key concepts. These great insights will help keep you on top of the bull!

CHAPTER VII

Freeway Speech

*I*f I could have had a voice recorder in my possession every time I've delivered a speech going down the freeway at 70 plus mph, I seriously doubt that the leader of any company or country would be able to top me. At those times my message is so articulate, so precise, so direct, and—of *course—so convincing, that no thinking person would possibly disagree with what I am saying. And certainly they would buy whatever it is I am selling.*

Too often, unfortunately, my freeway speeches and the speeches I actually make to an audience aren't anything alike. I get up to speak with a carefully constructed masterpiece in my back pocket. I know that I'm about to knock it out of the park. Then I begin speaking. Something happens...and it's not good. I forget parts of what I wanted to say, and I don't articulate other parts with the precision and passion I was hoping for. I can feel the downhill slide beginning to occur, and I'm powerless to stop it. Maybe you know what I'm talking about.

My great masterpiece has become so screwed up that I feel like I've lost my way. I'm definitely not on the freeway any longer. Now, at best, I'm parked on a side street desperately trying to figure out how to get back onto the freeway ramp. The speech started out nicely, but I'm beginning to pick up signs of trouble.

First, there is the body language from people in the audience. Yawns, people looking at their watches, or texting on their cell phones are sure signs that the freeway speech has departed. And the speech that has taken its place is leaving the listeners with confused looks on their face and mounting disinterest in what I'm saying. When I have gotten to this point in a speech, I am officially screwed. There's just no way around it.

The almost comical part is when I've looked back on talks like these and said to myself, "Really? Are you freaking kidding? Did I really just say that?" Or better, "Did I just get away with it? I sure hope so." Afterward, I've driven back down the road and looked at people in the cars next to me. I've wondered what they were thinking, if they were rehearsing their own speeches. I've wanted to honk and say, "Pull over and let's rehearse this together, because I know you're thinking about what you're going to say, and most of all how you're going to say it."

The freeway speech is one of the most positive times of your life. You're the only one listening to your bullshit, you're the only one who needs to believe it, and it sounds really, really good. When you pull in to wherever you're going, as you're getting out of your car, you should feel cocky and on top of the world. You're about to knock them dead with your freeway speech.

I love talking and I love speaking, and as my children say, I love preaching. One of my girls tells me I should be a preacher or run for President. It's nice she feels that way about her daddy. I make freeway speeches all the time. But I did deliver a speech to an audience one day that I'd like to share with you.

It was at Stephen F. Austin State University in Nacogdoches, Texas, and the topic was how to find a job in this day and age. There were three hundred students in the auditorium, as well as my oldest daughter. I said, "When you are out there, shake hands with folks you don't know and introduce yourself. Talk to people in the elevator, meet the siblings of friends, and get to know the parents of people you go home with on the weekends. Don't forget to shake the greeter's hand at Walmart and make someone feel good."

After I ended the speech, a young man stood up and said, "You've been in the insurance business a long time. Do you have any regrets?" I told him no. I said, "Regrets make you lose sleep. However, I've made my share of mistakes, and you should learn from those." Then a young lady in front stood up and asked, "So what was one of your mistakes?" I replied, "Not having Plan B in my pocket the day I was fired. Be sure to have a Plan B. As a pilot I can tell you that Plan B will come in handy and will be your saving grace in life." I had stayed on the freeway that day. As we were flying back, my daughter said, "Dad, you were good." Wow! What a compliment from a thirteen-year-old. She got the message, and she had the power to tell her Dad how she felt. That day put joy in my life because I had said what I wanted to say and made someone happy.

Be sure to enjoy moments like this, because all too often your speech, your presentation, or your attempts to communicate aren't going to leave you feeling that way. On the way home, you'll make another freeway speech consisting of all the things you should have said. If only the freeway speech and the actual speech could always be the same. I've learned that they're not; so, since that day, I've never changed that speech.

CHAPTER VIII

Real-World Smarts

I've discovered over the years that there is a big difference between "book smarts" and "street smarts." Book smarts are what we get in school, and there is a very real and valuable place for them. Street smarts are what we learn through the ups and downs of real life. In *the business world, I promise you, it is street smarts that win the day.*

Charles Sykes has written a great book entitled *50 Rules Kids Won't Learn in School: Real-World Antidotes to Feel-Good Education*. These concepts are often erroneously attributed to a graduation speech given by Bill Gates, but Sykes is the originator. Here are just a few of the many great lessons he lists:

> **Rule 1:** Life is not fair. Get used to it! The average teenager uses the phrase "It's not fair" 8.6 times a day.
>
> **Rule 2:** The real world will not care as much about your self-esteem as your school does. It'll expect you to accomplish something before you feel good about yourself.
>
> **Rule 3:** If you think your teacher is tough, wait till you get a boss. He doesn't have tenure, so he tends to be a bit edgier. When you screw up he's not going to ask you how you feel about it.
>
> **Rule 4:** Flipping burgers is not beneath your

dignity. Your grandparents had a different word for burger flipping...they called it opportunity.

Rule 5: If you mess up, it's not your parents' fault; so don't whine about your mistakes, learn from them.

Rule 6: Before you were born, your parents weren't as boring as they are now. They got that way from paying your bills, cleaning your clothes, and listening to you talk about how cool you thought you were. So before you save the rain forest from the parasites of your parent's generation, try delousing the closet in your own room.

Rule 7: Your school may have done away with winners and losers, but life has not. In some schools they have abolished failing grades and they'll give you as many times as you want to get the right answer. This doesn't bear the slightest resemblance to anything in real life.

Rule 8: Life is not divided into semesters. You don't get summers off and very few employers are interested in helping you find yourself. Do that on your own time.

Rule 9: Television is not real life. In real life

people actually have to leave the coffee shop and go to jobs.

Rule 10: Be nice to nerds. Chances are you'll end up working for one.

Book smarts are important and will always have their place. But real-world smarts get you ahead on the streets and in the boardroom.

CHAPTER IX

Who's Your Caddy?

I can't think of a day I didn't think about golf. When I was a young boy, my dad would call me his "Country Club Swinger," and at school they ribbed me because all I wanted to do was play golf— which wasn't easy in the blue-collar town of Dickinson. I wanted to look and play

*just like my grandpa—a man who looked
like golf incarnate. When he died, I was
fortunate enough to inherit his sweaters and golf clubs, Spalding Fluid Fills.
I wanted to be the best golfer in the world.
So I looked like one. My polyester pants
and my IZOD sweaters beat more guys on
the first tee than you could ever imagine.*

I ate golf balls for breakfast from age four until
about 1986, when I met my wife. That was the last
year I was in contention for a major title. On the first
round of the Houston City Amateur I shot a 69. I
invited my girlfriend (now my wife) to come watch
the second round. After looking over toward the cart
she was riding in, and seeing her asleep, I realized
that if I planned a life with her, my golf days would
be tapered. That smooth 84 I shot that day after bird-
ieing the first three holes humbled me.

As time went on, I didn't lose my appetite for the
game, I just found another interest. And I came to
terms with the undeniable realities that I wasn't as

good as I thought I was and I did not have to go for my opponent's jugular each time I stood on the tee. I've met some people on the course who have not come to these conclusions. I may have out-dressed many of them, but they had that burning look in their eyes and they were pointed at my jugular. I won a lot of money matches but I never conquered the club championship at any club where I was a member. But, golf has remained an integral part of my life and has been a tremendous teacher for me.

Walking a golf course, like walking a shoreline, reminds me that life is an individual game, often played against all odds. But as in golf, our greatest opponent in life is not the conditions on the outside but the person on the inside. I heard once that "The only victims in life are children, the rest of us are volunteers." Sooner or later we all come to recognize that we are the ones who have signed up to play the eighteen holes called life. Nobody else signed us up or took away our clubs. It is our dreams, habits, expectations, desires, neuroses, strengths, and weaknesses that combine to determine—more than anything else—what the eighteen holes of our life will be like.

When I reminisce about the times I walked down the manicured fairways of life, or found myself in the rough, or another tough position, I become keenly aware of something. There weren't many folks walking beside me or behind me to step up and help me get out of the mess I was in. Looking up in the trees, I never saw any money hanging off the limbs or people coming out of the bushes to say, "Follow me, and I'll get you out of here and take you to where you need to be." But, that's not the whole of the story, either.

During those times there actually have been a few people beside me. And though they couldn't play my round for me, they have carried my clubs better than anyone you've ever seen in the final round of any major tournament on TV. I'm not talking about the people who have carried my clubs and navigated me down the fine golf courses that I have had the privilege to play around the world. I'm talking about those few dear souls who were there when I had blisters on my feet and was so tired that I was ready to throw in the towel, who were there for me when I didn't think I could finish the course.

This thing called life is a kind of golf course. As I've played golf over the years I have had a few caddies and coaches who have helped to perfect my game. From my caddies Melvin and Breezy, to golf's greatest teaching professionals, Butch and Dick Harmon, I have been blessed to have some of the very best in my corner. But what I'm really talking about is those individuals who have been willing to stand behind me and beside me on the toughest course of all—the fairway of life.

I know who my caddies are, because they have walked through the fairways with me and navigated me through the toughest rough I have ever encountered. I am so very fortunate to have my wife, my children, my mom and my dad. Along with them are my brother, my cousin JR, and my grandparents. I also have several special friends: Adger, Riedel, Mandola, Everett Bernal, Bruce Whitaker, my dog Sport 1, and my pastor Jim Jackson. I'll never forget the barrel laughs from Jody Norris, and folks like Jesse Brown, William and Chris Townsend, Rebecca Morris, and all my daughters' friends who made me laugh. Others that come to mind are Dwight

Edwards, my Aunt Opel, Kay Rizzo, my cousin Ann, and Danny Gowen with his pickles. Also Bill Worthington, Chris Stobaugh, Bill Mosley, Matt Rotan, Leigh Ellis, my flight instructor Maybelle Fletcher, Allan Bailey, Frank Prisco, John Kafka, Amy Noles, Tom Overstreet, Billy Corbin, and so many more. I am forever grateful to these individuals who have been the best life-caddies one could ever hope for.

I know that's not many, and that's usually the case in most people's lives. But one or more of the individuals I just mentioned have been with me through every challenge I've met on that big course called life. Let me encourage you to do something. Look around to see who's carrying your clubs. Or better yet, who would be willing to walk beside you and share your burden? Think about the roughs and the fairways you've encountered so far. Who has been there? Name them specifically; maybe even write them down.

Why? When the band has finished playing and the lights have gone off, who will be there to help you get to the green or back in the fairway? Ask yourself before you tee off, "What do I plan on making on this hole?" Then look around to see who can help you make that score. No matter where you are on the course of life, ask the question, "Who's my caddy?" Who is it that knows what it takes to play the hole you're on and will help you to make that final putt. Life is tough enough on its own. Thank God that He places caddies along the way to help us. Be sure to be humble enough to let them carry your clubs now and then. Odds are they'll enjoy the opportunity.

CHAPTER X

A Mayonnaise Jar & Two Beers

A *friend sent me this bit of wisdom. It has served me well over the years, so I pass it on to you.*

When things in your life seem almost too much to handle, when twenty-four hours in a day are not enough, remember the mayonnaise jar and the two beers.

A professor stood before his philosophy class and had some items in front of him. When the class began, he wordlessly picked up a very large and empty mayonnaise jar and proceeded to fill it with golf balls. He then asked the students if the jar was full. They agreed that it was.

The professor then picked up a box of pebbles and poured them into the jar. He shook the jar lightly. The pebbles rolled into the open areas between the golf balls. He then asked the students again if the jar was full. They agreed it was.

The professor next picked up a box of sand and poured it into the jar. Of course, the sand filled up everything else. He asked once more if the jar was full. The students responded with a unanimous "Yes."

The professor then produced two beers from under the table and poured the entire contents into the jar effectively filling the empty space between the sand. The students laughed.

"Now," said the professor as the laughter subsided, "I want you to recognize that this jar represents your life. The golf balls are the important things—your family, your children, your health, your friends and your favorite passions—and if everything else was lost and only they remained, your life would still be full.

The pebbles are the other things that matter like your job, your house and your car.

The sand is everything else—the small stuff.

If you put the sand into the jar first," he continued, "there is no room for the pebbles or the golf balls. The same goes for life. If you spend all your time and energy on the small stuff you will never have room for the things that are important to you.

Pay attention to the things that are critical to your happiness. Spend time with your children. Spend time with your parents. Visit with grandparents. Take your spouse out to dinner. Play another eighteen. There will always be time to clean the house and mow the lawn.

Take care of the golf balls first—the things that really matter. Set your priorities. The rest is just sand."

One of the students raised her hand and inquired what the beer represented. The professor smiled and said, "I'm glad you asked. The beer just shows you that no matter how full your life may seem, there's always room for a couple of beers with a friend."

Great words of advice. I am so grateful for the times in my life that I really did put the golf balls first. I just wish that had been more often. As I look back over the years I recognize that the sand took up too much of my time and energy. But the professor is so right about the beer. Be sure to make time for a couple of beers with a friend. It helps keep perspective on the sand and the balls.

CHAPTER XI

Never Too Late

*O*ne of the most important lessons
I've ever learned in life is the need
to continue growing as a person.
*Regardless of age, regardless of past suc-
cess, regardless of past failure, we can all
attack life to the very end. A friend sent
me this story, and I love it.*

The first day of school our professor introduced him and challenged us to get to know someone we didn't already know. I stood up to look around when a gentle hand touched my shoulder. I turned around to find a wrinkled, little old lady beaming up at me with a smile that lit up her entire being. She said, "Hi handsome. My name is Rose. I'm eighty-seven years old. Can I give you a hug?"

I laughed and enthusiastically responded, "Of course you may!" and she gave me a giant squeeze. "Why are you in college at such a young, innocent age?" I asked. She jokingly replied, "I'm here to meet a rich husband, get married, and have a couple of kids."

"No seriously," I asked. I was curious what may have motivated her to be taking on this challenge at her age. "I always dreamed of having a college education, and now I'm getting one!" she told me.

After class we walked to the student union building and shared a chocolate milkshake. We became instant friends. Every day for the next three months we would leave class together and talk nonstop. I was always mesmerized listening to this "time machine" as she shared her wisdom and experience with me.

Over the course of the year, Rose became a campus icon, and she easily made friends wherever she went. She loved to dress up and she reveled in the attention bestowed upon her from the other students. She was living it up.

At the end of the semester we invited Rose to speak at our football banquet.

I'll never forget what she taught us. She was introduced and stepped up to the podium. As she began to deliver her prepared speech, she dropped her three-by-five cards on the floor. Frustrated and a little embarrassed she leaned into the microphone and simply said, "I'm sorry I'm so jittery. I gave up beer for Lent and this whiskey is killing me! I'll never get my speech back in order, so let me just tell you what I know."

As we laughed she cleared her throat and began, "We do not stop playing because we are old; we grow old because we stop playing. There are only four secrets to staying young, being happy and achieving success.

You have to laugh and find humor every day.

You've got to have a dream. When you lose your dreams, you die. We have so many people walking around who are dead and don't even know it!

There is a huge difference between growing older and growing up. If you are nineteen years old and lie in bed for one full year and don't do one productive thing, you will turn twenty years old. If I am eighty-seven years old and stay in bed for a year and never do anything I will turn eighty-eight.

Anybody can grow older. That doesn't take any talent or ability. The idea is to grow up by always finding opportunity in change. Have no regrets. The elderly usually don't have regrets for what we did, but rather for things we did not do. The only people who fear death are those with regrets."

She concluded her speech by courageously singing "The Rose."

She challenged each of us to study the lyrics and live them out in our daily lives.

At the year's end Rose finished the college degree she had begun all those years ago. One week after graduation Rose died peacefully in her sleep. Over two thousand college students attended her funeral in tribute to the wonderful woman who taught by example that it's never too late to be all you can possibly be.

Rose is a great example of how I want to live my life. And I hope you do, too.

Epilogue

I began our journey together by asking the question, "Do you have the bull or does the bull have you?" I hope these pages will help you take the bull by the horns and be able to say with the almost completely deaf Beethoven, "I will grab life by the throat!" As I've explained, my most important lessons have not been learned in a classroom or in pursuing a doctorate. They have most often been acquired in the school of hard knocks with professors I never saw coming—people, circumstances, and situations that God has used to weave the tapestry of my life. This tapestry has been the combination of good times, bad times, and many ordinary times. But every thread has had its place and purpose in the hand of the Master Weaver. Before we finish, I have a few closing thoughts to pass on.

Make the most of your memories. I go back to my memories often and have learned to enjoy memory lane better than most. My mother said that she enjoyed my memory better than hers, because she didn't remember things the way I did! Well, I tell it the best way I remember. One cannot live off memories of the past, but we certainly can benefit from them. We remember people and the traits they had that we want to emulate—or be sure to avoid. We remember how we made it through a particularly difficult situation, and that memory encourages us that we can do it again. Most of all, memory is a good thing because it teaches us what we learned through our mistakes. As I said before, there's no point in getting bit by the same dog twice. We can't change history but we can use it to help us change the future.

Take full advantage of other people's stories. I love having lunches when I get to hear great stories from those who have the wisdom to direct me through uncharted waters or give me a perspective I never considered. As I've shared in these pages, other people's lives and wisdom have helped shape me.

You have more to offer than you realize. When you are willing to share what has happened to you, others will be blessed far more than you probably realize. When someone younger than you says, "Tell me the time when…," realize that you have a golden teaching opportunity before you. Take full advantage of it. I love it when my daughters request my stories, because I know they are interested and are listening.

Life is anything but simple and predictable. Get used to it. Nobody ever said life was fair. Or that it was predictable. Or easy. But life is a wonderful gift to be experienced with everything in us. We have one life to leave this a better world than the one we entered. In spite of its inevitable heartaches, confusions, and setbacks, make the most of it.

The balance you create will keep the ripples from swamping your boat. The vast majority of life is about balancing two seemingly opposite truths or realities. Here are just a few:

1. Time at work vs. time with the family.
2. Spending money today vs. saving money for the

future.

3. Knowing when to tell your loved one how she or he irritates you vs. being patient and not making an issue of it.

4. Time spent in recreation vs. time spent working.

All of these are necessary tensions in a life that is well lived. Balance is the key; knowing which of these seeming opposites should take place when.

Personal change is good, but you will never change other people. We cannot change anyone but ourselves. Coming to terms with this is a definite milestone in anyone's life. We can encourage others, warn them, teach them, even plead with them, but we can never change them. And the more energy we spend trying to change others, the more we reduce the amount of energy available to make our own changes.

Know that enemies are stepping-stones and you will get through them to live for another day. No one makes it through life without having enemies. In fact, the more significantly we live our lives, the more enemies we will probably gain. But they really are your stepping-stones to becoming a better person and discovering things in life you never would otherwise.

Plan B makes you. So much of life is doing the second-best thing; that thing which was your second choice because your top choice didn't pan out. And you will find many times that your second choice ended up being the best choice when all the cards are played. If Plan A is the only card we have in our hand, we're setting ourselves up for big trouble.

Without an idea in your pocket and faith in your heart, you only exist. Life was not meant to be a mere existence but an assault. Jack London wrote,

"I would rather be ashes than dust! I would rather that my spark should burn out in a brilliant blaze than it should be stifled by dry-rot. I would rather be a superb meteor, every atom of me in magnificent glow, than a sleepy and permanent planet. The function of man is to live, not to exist. I shall not waste my days trying to prolong them. I shall use my time."

It's hard to put it better than that!

Whatever joy you can put into another's life will come back to you. There is an inevitable boomerang effect in life. What we throw out to others tends to come back to us as well. For better or worse. Be reckless in your generosity and concern for others and you will end up gaining far more than you gave away.

Listen to your gut when it speaks. This doesn't mean that you will always do what your gut-level instinct is telling you, but very often it is right. There are times when our heart knows something that our mind cannot quite put into words. Listen to that part deepest within you; it is often whispering better advice than you might think.

Be yourself. This is my closing thought. Oscar Wilde put it so well, "Be yourself, everyone else is already taken." I love that! There is a song only you can sing, a poem only you can write, a niche only you can fill. Don't try to play someone else's part, play your own, unique role to the hilt. Let the world see the deepest colors within you. You own the bull, now it's time to let it know who's on top!

Epilogue

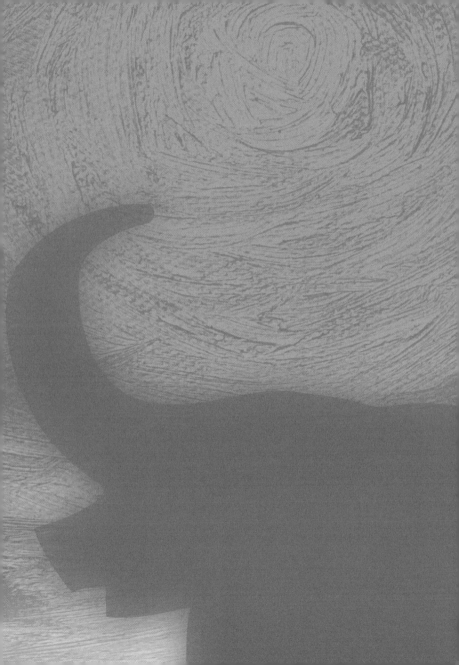

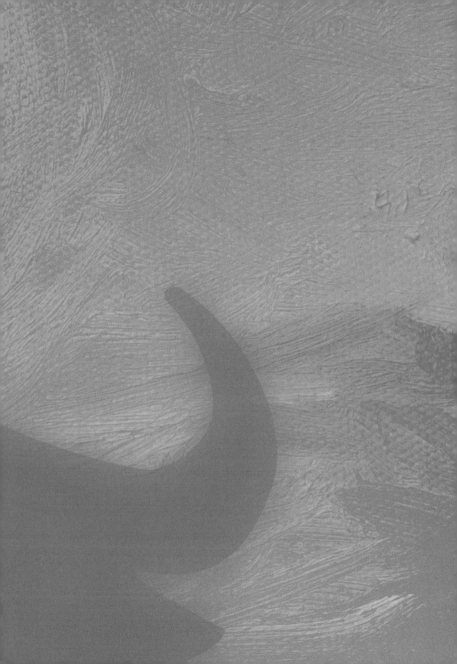